From Rob Roy's
The Wonderful
Wizard of OZ

Toto

©1985 Rob Roy Productions

From Rob Roy's
The Wonderful
Wizard of OZ

Dorothy Gale

©1985 Rob Roy Productions

From Rob Roy's
The Wonderful
Wizard of OZ · The Scarecrow
©1985 Rob Roy Productions

From Rob Roy's
The Wonderful
Wizard of OZ · The TinWoodman
©1985 Rob Roy Productions

From Rob Roy's
The Wonderful
Wizard of OZ

The Cowardly
Lion

©1985 Rob Roy Productions

From Rob Roy's
The Wonderful
Wizard of OZ

The
Wizard of
OZ

©1985 Rob Roy Productions

From Rob Roy's
The Wonderful
Wizard of OZ
The Good Witch
of the North

©1985 Rob Roy Productions

From Rob Roy's
The Wonderful
Wizard of OZ
BOQ
The Munchkin

©1985 Rob Roy Productions

From Rob Roy's The Wonderful Wizard of OZ · A Munchkin
©1985 Rob Roy Productions

From Rob Roy's The Wonderful Wizard of OZ · A Munchkin
©1985 Rob Roy Productions

From Rob Roy's
The Wonderful
Wizard of OZ • Queen of the Field Mice

©1985 Rob Roy Productions

From Rob Roy's
The Wonderful
Wizard of OZ • Mrs. Stork

©1985 Rob Roy Productions

From Rob Roy's
The Wonderful
Wizard of OZ • Field Mice

©1985 Rob Roy Productions

From Rob Roy's
The Wonderful
Wizard of OZ

The Soldier with the
Green Whiskers

©1985 Rob Roy Productions

From Rob Roy's
The Wonderful
Wizard of OZ

The
Guardian
of the
Gate

©1985 Rob Roy Productions

the base for the gate is on a following page

the
base for
the Trees
is on a
following
page

From Rob Roy's
The Wonderful
Wizard of OZ

©1985 Rob Roy Productions

The Forest Monster

©1985 Rob Roy Productions

The Fighting Trees

From Rob Roy's
The Wonderful
Wizard of OZ

attach this flap to the back of
the Fighting Trees

attach this flap to the back of the gate

From Rob Roy's
The Wonderful
Wizard of OZ · the Emerald City Gate

©1985 Rob Roy Productions

Mr. Joker

©1985
Rob Roy Productions

From Rob Roy's
The Wonderful
Wizard of OZ · The
Sun Bear

©1985 Rob Roy Productions

From Rob Roy's
The Wonderful
Wizard of OZ · The Hungry Tiger

©1985 Rob Roy Productions

From Rob Roy's
The Wonderful Wizard of OZ
Hammer-Head
©1985 Rob Roy Productions

From Rob Roy's
The Wonderful Wizard of OZ
Hammer-Head
©1985 Rob Roy Productions

From Rob Roy's
The Wonderful Wizard of OZ
Hammer-Head
©1985 Rob Roy Productions

The China
Milkmaid
©1985 Rob Roy Productions

The Porcelain
Princess
©1985 Rob Roy Productions

From Rob Roy's
The Wonderful
Wizard of OZ

Glinda the Good
©1985 Rob Roy Productions

The China Cow
©1985 Rob Roy Productions

From Rob Roy's
The Wonderful
Wizard of OZ · **Uncle Henry**

©1985 Rob Roy Productions

From Rob Roy's
The Wonderful
Wizard of OZ · **Aunt Em**

©1985 Rob Roy Productions

Home Sweet Home

The Wonderful Wizard of Oz was written by L. Frank Baum in 1899. Five generations have loved the many versions of his story told in books, on stage, in film, and on television. For those who love the Land of Oz as much as we do, we dedicate this book.

The Story of The Wonderful Wizard of OZ

Dorothy Gale lived on a Kansas prairie farm with her Aunt Em and Uncle Henry and her dog, Toto. One day a fierce cyclone carried Dorothy and Toto to the Land of Oz, where they were greeted by the Good Witch of the North and the Munchkins. Dorothy was told to follow the Yellow Brick Road to the Emerald City, where the Wizard of Oz would help her return home. On her way, Dorothy met the Scarecrow, who wanted a brain; the Tin Woodman, who wanted a heart; and the Cowardly Lion, who needed courage. They joined her in her journey to ask the Wizard for his help. Together the new friends had adventures with the Kalidah, the Stork, and the Field Mice before arriving safely at the Emerald City of Oz.

The Guardian of the Gate and the Soldier with the Green Whiskers led them to the Great Oz. The Wizard said he would help them if they could destroy the Wicked Witch of the West. Downhearted but determined, Dorothy and her friends headed West, where they were attacked by the winged Monkeys under orders from the Witch. Taken to the Witch's castle and trapped in a corner, Dorothy accidentally melted the Witch with a bucket of water. The grateful Monkeys helped the heroes return to the Wizard. But the Wizard turned out to be a fake; he was a humbug from Omaha. Still, he was able to help the Scarecrow, the Tin Woodman, and the Lion, but in trying to help Dorothy he was carried off in a hot-air balloon, leaving her stranded.

Once again discouraged, the friends left the Emerald City and headed South to see if Glinda the Good could help Dorothy get home. On the way they met the Fighting Trees, the China People, the Hammer-Heads, and the Sun Bear and Hungry Tiger—whom the Cowardly Lion bravely rescued from the Forest Monster. At Glinda's palace, Dorothy learned that she could get home by knocking her heels together three times and saying, "Take me home to Aunt Em." And in just three winks of an eye, she and Toto were home again with Aunt Em and Uncle Henry.

Instructions

Leaving a white border, or following exactly around the edge, carefully cut out the figures and bases. For extra rigidity, you may want to glue flat toothpicks or strips of cardboard to the back of the figures. Fold the base as indicated along the dotted lines, weight the base (pennies work well), and glue the outside tab to the back of the figure. When the glue is dry, the wonderful characters of Oz are ready to journey with you through hours of adventure.

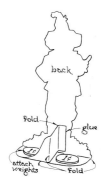

About the artists

Rob Roy Productions is a creative group of artists and animators headed by Rob Roy MacVeigh. In *The Wonderful Cut-Outs of Oz*, they are pleased to present this advance look at the cast of their forthcoming animated presentation of *The Wonderful Wizard of Oz*, based on L. Frank Baum's original classic, and the early Oz illustrations by W. W. Denslow and John R. Neill.

35 Stand-up figures from the Magical Land of Oz!

All the characters from L. Frank Baum's enchanted kingdom
(including Dorothy, the Scarecrow, the Tin Woodman,
the Cowardly Lion, and many more) are here waiting
to be adopted by you!

Crown Publishers, Inc. • One Park Avenue • New York, New York 10016

ISBN 0-517-55916-1